Hi ... I'm Ga

Ok Girls this book is just for you, as it is all about that strange alien life form that causes us so many problems "**Boys**".

The following pages will give ideas on:

**Meeting Them, Managing Them
& all that Love Stuff,**

Want to know more? read on ......

Published by
REARDON PUBLISHING
PO Box 919, Cheltenham, Glos, GL50 9AN.
Website: www.reardon.co.uk
Tel: 01242 231800
Email: reardon@bigfoot.com

Copyright © 2010
Reardon Publishing

A Gabby Guide
Written by
Rachel Hill

ISBN 1-874192-04-9
ISBN (13) 9781874192046

Art Work by Manga Artist
Heby Sim

Layout and Design by
Nicholas Reardon

www.gabby-guides.com

Printed In England

Start Here

The unknown world of boys has been a problem that has plagued girl-kind for many a century. What do you say to them? Which ones should you avoid? And what is going on in that little brain of theirs when they look at you?

If only they came with a manual or something…If only someone had kidnapped one of these boys, smuggled them into the garage and threatened them with curling tongs to give out all the answers…If only they'd written it all up in a lovely step by step guide that's split into five easy stages, taking you from finding the right kind of boy for you right up to ending a relationship and starting all over again.

Well someone has! I'm not saying it's me and I'm guessing whoever did do it isn't going to want to be taking much credit for it. All I'm saying is I have the information under non-suspicious circumstances and you can wave goodbye to worrying about what kind of shoes to wear for a date or how to make the first move; it has all been covered.

But how do you use this brilliant little tool? Well, if you want you can read through each chapter and follow the advice you find in it step-by-step. But there's also a handy content list at the beginning of each stage so you can skip to any section you want to read about.

Whoever it is who does have that poor boy tied to a chair by his shoelaces has done us all a big favour. You can thank me later. ;)

Great! It's on to the first chapter then…

Stage One

Title: This is where it all begins!

Difficulty level: Rather difficult.... certainly not for the faint-hearted!

Description: whilst this could possibly be the most exciting area of your journey it's also one of the most nerve-racking because it involves talking to hot guys! Luckily there are some sneaky tips to make things easier and it's recommended that tasks are carried out with the help of your friends! By the end you'll be an expert in spotting potential boyfriends, starting conversations and making a winning first impression.

Contents:

Welcome	05
The Boy Catalogue	06
Brain training	28
Grabbing his ...attention	28
Outfits for all occasions	33
Putting together a winning team	34
Quick re-cap	37
Checkout	38

Welcome!

To begin with it would help if we found out a little bit more about those strange creatures we call boys. They can be a bit tricky to understand so it's best to liken them to something most girls know a little bit more about. Like shoes. Yes, boys are a little like shoes.

Why? Well... They can be useful. But mainly...

* *They are nice to look at.*

* *Getting the right one can be a lovely accessory to an outfit.*

* *There are times when you couldn't do without them.*

* *And there are times when you'd rather do without them.*

* *Get the wrong ones and they can hurt.*

* *There are many types and often the ones that look the nicest are completely inpractical.*

Like shoe shopping you need to get to know what's out there before you make your final purchase. Your first task, should you choose to accept it, is one of girl kind's most notable hobbies...with a twist... boy shopping! To make things even easier, included here is the very first boy catalogue giving you an extensive look into all the boys on the market.

Good luck and happy shopping!

The Boy Catalogue
spring/summer/autumn/winter

Band Guy

If there's anything that makes a boy instantly attractive, it's being in a band. There's something about a long-haired rocker with a guitar in his hand that can turn any girl's legs to jelly. But they're not the easiest of guys to catch so read on to find out how to get your hands on one!

Where to find them

Band guys are easy to spot because when they're not on stage performing their latest "big hit" they can be found perusing the local music shop for their fave bands new album. However, unfortunately they're not just going to land at your doorstep, so here's the three top places to find yourself a band guy:

*   GIGS! These places are a goldmine when looking for the band type. You can find them onstage or in the crowd and it's the perfect place to strike up a conversation about things you'll have in common.

*   All bands need decent instruments to start off so head down to your nearest instrument shop and you're bound to find a couple of hotties.

*   Bands also need some inspiration for their songs so they'll be likely to be checking out the CD aisles so give the music shop a try.

Band Guy

*   For the shy girl the Internet is an absolute lifesaver when it comes to dating. Sites like Facebook and Myspace let you set up your own profile page where you can make the perfect first impression. Band guys especially love these sites because they can promote their band so you'll be spoilt for choice! Just remember to be safe in case the person you're talking to turns out not to be who you thought they were.

How to start a convo

This is probably the easier type of guy to strike up a winning conversation with because you already have a heads up on what they're interested in ...music! But talking to any guy can still be hard so here's a few tricks to help you get started:

*   Just after his band have finished performing, run up to him and say how much you love his music and if they have any demo CDs. Any boy loves to hear how great he is so he'll be dying to talk to you.

*   If you spot him looking through the CD racks casually walk over to where he's standing and start looking through the CDs beside him, make sure it looks genuine though. After about 30 seconds or so sigh loudly and ask him if he knows where "insert name of popular band" new album is. He'll be so glad he can finally put his extensive music knowledge to use there is no way he'll say no when you go to ask for his phone number.

*   If you've got an instrument handy ask him if he does music lessons. What better chance to get to know each other than in an hour of one on one teaching?

*   Start up your own band. Its great fun and once you start gigging you can ask if his band wants to do a gig with you, and as a bonus you'll finally get to see what it's like to go backstage!

The Geek

He's cute, loveable and ever so sweet but not everyone can see past his not-so cool exterior so he's labelled a bit of a geek. But sometimes it can be fun to let out your inner nerd and there comes a time in every girl's life when she can no longer resist the boyish charms of a geek. And what's the big deal anyway, as long as you're happy with him who cares what everyone else thinks!

Where to find them

*   Hmm, these guys can be hard to find because they tend to prefer staying at home, finishing homework, which can be a problem. But be patient and it's only a matter of time before one of them dares to venture out!

*   You're most likely to find a geek huddled in the corner of the library. It's a geek haven, full of books, computers etc.

*   The next best thing is any form of after-school club. A few of the best ones to try are chess club, computer club, and science club.

*   Join a study group or reading group, just make sure you'll be willing to sit through hours of lectures without falling asleep!

*   Take up a new interest in modern art and visit galleries or take a trip round all the museums nearby.

*   As a last resort, try any of the following: Internet cafes, bookshops, game shops or anywhere connected with learning.

*   However the best place to find a geeky guy is at school where you're bound to find an infinite supply of bookworms!

How to start a convo

Once you've spied your geek you need to know what to say to him. They tend not to be the most outgoing boys so its unlikely they'll make the first move.

*   Ask him to mentor you. Even if you know the subject better than him pretend you're struggling and ask him if he could help you in exchange for your email address!

*   Next time you spot him in a bookshop pretend to be looking at the same type of book as him and ask him if he knows anything about the previous work of the author. You'll sound extremely clever which is probably exactly his type of girl!

*   Grab a friend and start talking loudly about some controversial topic about politics (get info from a newspaper or the Internet) so he can hear. Eventually he'll get so caught up in the argument that he'll just have to join in.

The Geek

Sporty Guy

Football, tennis, basketball...he likes them all. This guy's first love is sport and unless you're a bit of a sports fetishist yourself it's unlikely you'll have that much in common at first, so it's advisable to start taking a bit of an interest in this kind of thing before you try and get to know him. That doesn't include just watching how hot he looks running around in shorts!

Where to find them

Do you have to even ask? If you want to find yourself a sporty guy you really don't have to look very far.

*   Any type of live game whether it is a footy match or a golf tournament it's guaranteed to be packed with the sporty kind. However getting in can be expensive so if you have a brother or friend who's in a sports team, take a sudden interest in their hobbies and go to "support". If you're lucky they'll introduce you to some of their team-mates!

*   Your second best bet is a sports centre where you might just stumble across a sporty guy brushing up on his skills. Flash him a grin and he might just come over to give you a game.

*   Sports shops tend to have a few sporty people in so next time you're getting new shoes spare five minutes to check it out.

*   For the truly dedicated, take up sports lessons. However much they try to convince you that they were born with it, sports guys have to learn their skills from somewhere!

Sporty Guy

How to start a convo

Well to be honest just anything to do with sport will suffice. For example:

*	Ask him to show you how to play. Golf works best for this one, as he'll have to put his arms round you to show you how to hit the ball.

*	...Or if you're a bit of a sports' master yourself challenge him to a game. Just be careful, however much he likes you he's not going to play nice, as he would never be able to live down the fact he got beat by a girl.

*	If you see him at a game, get a seat as close to him as possible. The next time someone scores shout and whistle like you're really excited by it (make sure it's the same team he's supporting) and while everyone's congratulating each other turn to him and say "well that was good wasn't it". If he's interested you'll be exchanging numbers before half time.

The Bad Boy

He's tough, a real bad ass and damn hot! For some reason girls seem to love a boy with a real sense of danger. Is it the challenge of trying to tame their rebellious ways, the thrill of living on the wild side or just how fit they look in their anti-fit jeans? Who knows but be careful when falling for a bad boy, it's unlikely they're ever going to play by the rules which could leave you broken hearted. You've been warned!

Where to find them

*   They're like most likely to be spending their time in school in detention. But when they're not stuck at home being grounded, they'll be spending their time driving about on their bike, graffitiing on walls and generally causing trouble.

*   However some bad boys like to channel their wild side into a hobby so be sure to check out the skate park, bike ramps or any other death- defying sport facilities.

How to start a convo

This is a toughie because they aren't typically big talkers but give them the right topics and they'll happily chat away!

*   Ask him about his latest all nighter/escape from police dogs/near- miss with the nasty next door neighbour. As he tells you laugh (appropriately) if it's a funny story or just look amazed. When he's finished give him a loud "wow". As we all know flattery gets you everywhere!

*   Make up your own awe-inspiring story about what you did at the weekend. Try to keep it realistic and tell your friends beforehand to avoid any "no you didn't" outbursts!

*   Offer to lend him your notes from the last lesson he missed because he was standing outside getting in trouble. He'll be grateful for any help he can get to get his parents off his back.

The Bad Boy

The Random Encounter

You're walking down the street/into a party/to your gran's and out of the corner of your eye you spot the most gorgeous guy you've ever seen. You know nothing about him but you just have to have him. Well now you can...

Where to find them

ANYWHERE! Literally a hot guy can walk past you anytime, anywhere which stands to reason for the rule - always look your best! You just never know when you're going to come across your dream boyfriend!

How to start a convo

*   If he's on his own, this makes him slightly easier to approach but also means he may be shy. Just make sure you go up to him by yourself, a giant group of girls is extremely intimidating for a boy by himself.

*   If he's with his mates, it'll be easier for him to talk to you but he might act differently because he'll be "showing off". Try to have the same number of friends with you as him so girl to boy ratio is equal, giving you a better chance to get him by himself (as you'll find out later on).

*   If you see him on the street ask him for the time or better still ask him for directions to a shop, if he's not busy he might walk you there!

The Random Encounter

*   If you see him at a party gives him loads of eye contact while you're dancing and smile.

*   If he still doesn't come over to talk to you, go and stand beside him. "Accidentally" knock into him and say sorry asking him if he's ok. If the replies yes then blab on about how silly the people beside you are for pushing you into him - anything to keep the conversation going! If he replies no then you're in a bit of trouble!

*   If you see him at the park pull another one of your "accidental" collisions with him. As you apologise look at him in a confused face and ask him whether he goes to your school because you are sure you recognise him.

*   Anywhere else The best way to guarantee his attention is to just be upfront. Walk over and say, "Hi what's your name". It's definitely going to get his attention.

Product Recall!

The following products are no longer on sale in the catalogue and should you find one avoid and warn all fellow girls to keep well away.

Smoky Joe

How to spot one:

*   Can be difficult to see their face as they are often hidden behind a cloud of smoke.

*   Known most notably for their trademark ciggie hanging off their lip.

*   Have perfected the art of blowing smoke circles.

*   Says hi to his "friends" on street corners.

*   Is into gardening... in his loft.

*   Follows Pete Doherty as a fashion icon.

*   While he may look like he has puppy dog eyes it's probably just because he has unusually large pupils most of the time.

*   Could be mistaken for a bad boy but is in fact a sad boy, a very, very sad boy for thinking his "habits" are cool. They really aren't and you'll probably find that when he's not taking something he's pretty boring. Not to mention the fact that he'll look like your granddad in about 10 years time.

SMOKY JOE

Mr Know-it-all

Warning...

Now there's nothing wrong with being confident, but this guy has trouble getting his head through the door because it's so big.

*   His ego is the eighth wonder of the world...well at least he thinks it is.

*   Quite good-looking but he certainly knows it.

*   Self-proclaimed "God's gift to girl-kind".

*   Is good at...well from what he says just about everything.

*   His idea of Saturday entertainment is listening to the sound of his own voice.

The Player

You know you've found one if he:

*   Aspires to live in the Playboy mansion and wears pyjamas whenever he can.

*   Winks so often you're not sure whether it is a facial tick.

*   Has trouble with remembering names, thinks everyone is called "babe"...even the guys.

*   Has even more trouble with maintaining eye contact, they always seem to drift southwards.

*   Thinks being "faithful" is cheating with one girl at a time.

*   Never seen without his arms around his "girls".

*   Thinks Akon's song "Smack that" is romantic.

The Gamer

A guy's allowed a hobby but look out in case he:

*   Has every form of electronic entertainment available.

*   Has posters of computer cartoons instead of wallpaper.

*   His eyes almost look square and he has premature arthritis in his thumbs.

*   Talks in "html" code.

*   Instead of birthdays he marks video game release dates on his calendar.

*   Thinks Tomb Raider is factual history and considers getting to level three as an achievement worthy of going on his CV.

The Gamer

Next

Wow, that's a lot of guys! But before you go to do some serious browsing, you're going to need confidence and probably a lot of it. It's surprising how difficult it can be to utter the word "hi" to someone new ...especially someone hot! Unfortunately with most girls confidence is in rather short supply, so listen up and soon you'll be brimming with the stuff.

Brain Training

Most of us worry about how to talk to new people especially when those people are guys. First impressions are important but don't spend precious time fretting over the petty stuff that he probably won't notice. Under the strictest scientific research, I've compiled a list to give you the low down on what boys will notice and what they will not.

Grabbing his...attention

As you've just seen, boys are definitely not like girls and while you're obsessing about that spot on your nose, he's probably not even looking at your face! We can use this information to our advantage by looking at what boys will notice before they've even spoken to you and how to get him to notice you!

1.   Your body - in particular your boobs and/or bum. Well boys will be boys! So stand with one leg crossed in front of the other, as it will give your body a flattering outline.

2.   Your face- despite common belief, doing the moody pout you've been perfecting is pretty much the same as writing a do not disturb sign across your forehead. Try giving a hearty smile in his direction once in a while so you look a bit less Cruella and little more Cinderella! Eyes are also a big pulling feature so be sure to give him lots of eye contact.

3.   Your clothes- although it's superficial, boys can tell a lot about your personality from your clothes, not designer labels or how expensive they are but the style! For example if you're wearing a band tee he'll know you're into music. Wearing dangerously low cut tops and bum showing mini skirts will get his attention, but not for the right reasons and chances are you'll look like you're trying too hard.

4.   Are you with a boyfriend - after being dumbstruck by your fabulousness his instincts will kick in telling him to get closer to you. Obviously he has to check that he's not going to get his lights punched out if he makes a move so he'll be making sure you're not taken.

5.   Are you interested - eventually he'll realise that his complicated plan designed to make him look as smooth as James Bond is only going to work if you like him as well. But remember boys just don't do subtle, if you're interested let him know!

Getting the wrong sort of attention:

There are of course other ways to get his attention, along with the rest of the population within a 5-mile radius. But unless there's a boy with a really strange sense of humour nearby or you truly have no shame then these techniques should be saved for drama club only:

Dramatically swooning (sound effects included) in an attempt to fall into his arms, which most likely will result in a serious case of concussion.

Sporting your Christine Aguilera-style buttless chaps and bikini top around your local supermarket will certainly turn heads.

Wearing giant oversized sunnies midwinter and getting a mob of "fans" to run after you begging you for your autograph (just remember to make sure you know what you're actually pretending to be famous for in case he asks).

Training your brain

Now you know what he is thinking it's time to take a look at what you're thinking because one of the most confidence crushing things of all is that little voice in your head and you need to teach yourself to ignore all negative things it comes out with. For every nasty comment that comes in you need to tell it to change it into something positive.

Naughty voice says: He's never going to like you, you should just give up now

You hear: How could he not like you! You should give him a cheeky wink

Naughty voice says: You look so fat in those jeans and your face is looking decidedly spotty.

You hear: Woah, your butt looks fantastic in those jeans and your face is looking decidedly gorgeous.

Naughty voice says: He's too good for you, there's no way you could compare to the other girls who must like him.

You hear: You're too good for him! These other girls don't stand a chance.

Fake it till you make it

By now you should be feeling pretty sure of yourself.

But for those momentary lapses of confidence learn how to "fake it till you make it"

First you need to create a sort of fake persona, which in other words is the little more outgoing version of yourself. Give the "new you" a cool nickname to help you change from the shy you. Even celebrities like Beyonce use this trick, who uses her sassy alter ego "Sasha" while she's on stage.

Now imagine a situation you would normally feel very self-conscious in and picture yourself acting very confident. Remember what facial expressions you had and what tone of voice you used then try to imitate it.

(It might be easier to watch someone else who's pretty confident and then try to copy.)

When you're in your "new persona", keep your arms unfolded, your head up and a smile on your face. You'll look relaxed and friendly and after a while just standing in that position will make you feel instantly more confident.

Your 'new you' should talk loudly (enough so people can hear, not enough to cause deafness).

Try to hold back the giggles unless someone actually says something funny. Bouts of nervous laughter might give the game away.

So next time you need a bit of an ego boost call in your "other you". At least then if things go wrong you can blame it on someone else!

OK so you're feeling about as confident as Simon Cowell (hopefully without the need to wear your trousers round your chin). In fact clothes are a big thing in the girl world and looking good on the outside can really help you to feel good on the inside too. Only problem left is what do you wear?

Here to solve all your dressing dilemmas is personal stylist er…me.

Outfits for all occasions

For all those bellas looking for fellas you're going to need something that catches his eye. I am thinking bright colours and pinched in waistlines, so what could be more wonderful than a knee length, white dress? Something a little like zis I think.

Stylish cardigan (just in case it's cold!)

Belt around the waist to give you flattering curves.

Boots with a bit of heel.

White, dress to show off your feminine side.

Tip: if you don't feel comfortable wearing a dress then swap it for a long, flowing top and wear over drainpipe jeans.

FRIENDS

PUTTING TOGETHER A PULLING TEAM

Now you're almost ready to go, you know what you're looking for and you're looking fabulous but it's tough being alone. For double the fun grab all your friends and go out on the pull all together.

Pick your team wisely though. Here's a list of the type of girls who might be the most useful to take with you.

Name: **the chatty one**
Distinguishing features: talks a lot
Good for: keeping his friends occupied whilst you work your magic
Bad for: not letting you get a word in

Name: **the fashionable one**
Distinguishing features: always has the latest trends, has a lot of make-up
Good for: making sure you look your best at all times
Bad for: can be a little too critical of your appearance

Name: **the shoulder to cry on one**
Distinguishing features: good listener, enjoys helping people with their problems, always there when things get tough
Good for: helping you recover from embarrassing mishaps caused by you turning into a mumbling fool by a Brad Pitt look-alike
Bad for: can be negative

Name: **the joker**
Distinguishing features: makes jokes, laughs a lot, good sense of humour
Good for: making the whole experience a little more fun
Bad for: making inappropriate jokes at bad times

Name: **the loud mouth**
Distinguishing features: very outgoing, isn't afraid to say what she thinks
Good for: getting you noticed and beginning conversations when you're feeling shy
Bad for: being a bit embarrassing

Name: **the boy mate**
Distinguishing features: potential to grow a beard, doesn't wear skirts...er basically a boy
Good for: giving you advice on all things boy shaped
Bad for: making it look like you already have a boyfriend

However no matter how fashionable, chatty or funny these people maybe do not take them along:

Name: **the stunner**
Distinguishing feature: model like looks and never ending legs
Good for: making you feel like crap
Bad for: making you feel like crap

Name: **the whiner**
Distinguishing feature: not interested and moans till she gets her own way
Good for: making you go home early
Bad for: moaning on

Name: **the hermit**
Distinguishing feature: very shy, doesn't like talking to people
Good for: bringing down your confidence
Bad for: stopping you from talking to boys & the amazing vanishing trick!

Now you've got your team ready you need to know how to use it. This is just one of the ways your "pulling posse" can help you out. Nothing can up the fear factor like a massive group of boys. If you see someone you like but he happens to be surrounded by all his friends, use your team to get him by himself:

BEGIN WITH A LARGE GROUP OF BOYS.

Point out to your friends the boy who catches your eye and then assign each of the other boys to a member of the team. If you are outnumbered then get two of your friends to pair up and assign three or four guys to each pair.

Get your group to walk over to theirs and ask them something like the time or the directions to somewhere.

Using the tips from the boy catalogue get each girl or pair to strike up a conversation with their assigned guy, leaving the one you picked out.

Voila, your chosen guy is now ready and waiting for you to start up your own conversation with him.

Quick re-cap

The time has come for you to put all you've learnt into practice and get out there and meet some boys! So here's a quick recap over how to put what we've learnt into practice:

Pick what kind of guy you like the look of from the catalogue (if your not sure why not just give them all a try)

Make sure you're feeling confident and clued up about how to stand out from the crowd

Get yourself looking gorgeous

Teach your new skills to your mates

Get out there and meet some boys!

For every boy you meet ensure that you get enough information to fill in the following form.

Tip: It's probably a good idea to meet as many guys as you can at this point so you don't lay all your hopes on just one of them.

If you want to be really naughty, why not invest in a classic little black book to store all the details of the hot guys you meet for future reference.

Checkout

To order your "dream guy", just fill out the following form with his details and he will be dispatched to you very soon!

Name

Type

Age

Town/city

Phone number and/or email address

Should you have any problems with your product please do not hesitate to rip up the form and send him packing immediately.

Once you're all finished shopping you can carry on to stage two where the real fun begins.

"Now on to stage 2"

STAGE TWO

Title: Getting a little closer

Difficulty: Not too bad, well it's definitely a lot better than doing the housework!

Description: now to get to the important part, you know what kind of guy you're after, you've been meeting and greeting all week and now comes the tricky decision of picking who you want and take in your new found friendship on to new levels …. Simple. Or is it?

CONTENTS

Finding your target	*40*
Long distance vs. short distance	*41*
Do your research	*43*
Three's a crowd	*46*
Turning on the flirt	*48*
Does he like you?	*50*
Make it a date	*53*

First stage over and hopefully you're feeling spoilt for choice. Now that you've met a whole load of boys you can pick which one you think you most have a future with. But before you set your eye on someone there are a few details you need to check...

Finding your target

Is he single? You might be thinking that you can make him dump his current girlfriend or have already heard that things aren't going too well between them but until they are officially over then you should keep well away. You never know what's going to happen between them and waiting around for someone isn't fun and often ends up being a complete waste of time. If he cheats on her then he's certainly not worthy of your time: remember if he can do that to her, he can easily do that to you.

Is he off limits? The following guys are *STRICTLY OFF LIMITS:* someone known to cheat, someone with a violent temper, teachers, anyone double your age.

And these guys should be approached with caution: any of your friends' ex boyfriends, the best mate of your last boyfriend, someone who has turned you down before, the guy your best mate has been wanting to go out with for months.

Do you like him for the right reasons? If you are only after someone for any of the following reasons, you should seriously consider changing your mind as someone is bound to get hurt... and it could easily be you.

- *to make an ex jealous*
- *to win a bet*
- *for a joke*
- *for revenge*
- *just to prove you can get a boyfriend*

...And finally just a small note on fancying celebrities

They are perfect for hanging pictures of on your wall, drooling over on television, and Googling till you know more about them than probably they do. But while you may think that you two are destined to be together, devoting all your attention to a celebrity can be a bit of a waste of brain space! Chances are without all their stage make up and photo- shopped biceps they'll look more pasty than tasty. And who knows while you're spending all your time fixated on someone who doesn't even know you exist, you could be missing the very cute guy who lives just next door!

Any boys who don't fit the criteria you need to cross off your list before things go any further. You might also want to consider how easy it would be to keep in contact with him because this could affect a relationship later on. Committing to a long distance relationship can be very hard and isn't wise if you're after something serious. But this can be a hard one to call so let's look at the pros and cons.

Long distance relationships Vs short distance relationships

Reasons not to have a long distance relationship:

Reason 1 - The distance can put a strain on the relationship, you might have to travel a long way to see them and although you can keep in touch over emails and letters it's just not the same.

Reason 2 - You'll always have the worry that you don't know what he is doing on a day to day basis and not being around makes it easier for him to cheat- or of course make it easier for you to be distracted by someone else!

Reason 3 - Being far apart makes it difficult to go and enjoy the small things of being together like going round his house on a Friday night to watch DVD's together, going to parties with your very own escort and getting a cheer-up-hug after a bad day. It might start to feel like your missing out or worse, that you haven't really got a boyfriend at all.

Reason 4 - If you have an argument with him its easy to let things go and get out of hand because you don't see him face to face to sort things out.

However if you're not really after a long-term relationship or the distance is only temporary then maybe it's not such a bad idea. Long distance relationship's can work for some people and there's nothing to say you can't end things should you find they aren't working out. After all having a bit of distance has its advantages:

Reason 1 - When you do see him it will be extra special and you'll appreciate that time you have together a lot more.

Reason 2 - You have more time to spend doing other things without worrying that your being neglectful.

Reason 3 - As the saying goes "Distance makes the heart grow fonder"

Managed to narrow your list down to just one yet? Probably not. Getting to know them might help you make your final decision over who is best for you. If you already know who it is you want then all the better! Once the initial, first conversation is over you can also concentrate on showing him the real you. You'll only do this by talking to him LOTS! That's not saying turn into his second shadow but just as much as possible whilst not appearing on the verge of obsession. It's difficult to know when playing it cool turns into too cool but generally saying hi to him when you see him is good and hanging round outside his house for a couple of hours just to say hi is bad. If he's hanging out with his friends then try to join in a conversation with them as well so you look sociable. If you're having problems thinking of things to say then it might be helpful to do a bit of undercover work.

Do your research

Put your night goggles away, we're talking about his favourite type of music and who is friends are. Not what time he wakes up and the last ten phone calls he made! Doing a bit of research on things he likes helps you get to know what kind of guy he is and gives a few topics to talk about to prevent those mid-flirt mind blanks. Here's what information you should know:

Where he likes to hangout. If you know them, ask his mates where he likes to hang out and what sort of things he likes to do. Not only will this give you something to talk about but also you can plan a "surprise" meeting where you just happen to turn up at his favourite hangout!

What kind of music he likes. Look on any web sites or profile pages he has and see what you can work out from there. Perhaps he has a background wallpaper of his favourite band or musician. If so, see if you can get to listen to a couple of their songs or read up a little bit about who they are. Even if you find you don't like them it will at least give you something to argue over!

What his hobbies are. A good topic of conversation is always "what are you up to at the weekend". Try to ask this a couple of times (just not in the same week!) and pay close attention to his replies to see what kind of hobbies he has. This is particularly useful in seeing what you have in common.

His personality. This is the most important one and requires you to talk to him in person for a fairly long time (10-15 minutes at least). Does he come across as arrogant, bossy or bad tempered? Does he say nasty things about other people while you're with him? All these things are a bad sign that this isn't the kind of boy you want to get mixed up with. It's true that he could be just having a bad day but if your gut feeling tells you something's just not quite right then trust yourself and back away.

As you get to know him a little better you'll probably get to know about the other women in his life as well, most likely including his mother. However before you let your green eyed monster take over make sure you know what you're dealing with.

His ex

Very few boys still keep in contact with their ex-girlfriends and fewer still actually like them. The problem comes however when his ex is still hanging around for whatever reason and you're not quite sure whether things have completely fizzled out between them. In times like these, your first line of action is to try and judge who is the one keeping in touch. If it's her then you don't need to worry but if it's him then he might not be quite ready to get into another relationship. The important thing is to remember that the relationship didn't work and it's unlikely that it will work again. So give him some time and take things slowly.

Someone who fancies him

This all depends on whether or not you think he fancies her too. Does he talk to her a lot? Does he return her flirting? Have you ever heard anything about him liking her back? If any of the answers to these questions is a yes then maybe you might have a little bit to worry about. But before you give up hope ask yourself, if he likes her and she likes him why aren't they going out yet? Until they are an official couple there's no reason to think that he won't go out with you, so keep on flirting!

Someone who he fancies

This is probably the worst kind you can get. You might want to try and find out exactly how long he has liked her for and whether or not you think she is interested in him. If he's liked her for a long time then it might just be a case that he hasn't found anyone else in the meantime. This is your cue to enter and show him what he's been missing, which will of course make him forget that there ever was another girl. But if you think she might like him too then it's best to maybe look for another guy. Whatever you do don't venture into the dark territory of sabotaging their relationship, that includes things like spreading nasty rumours about her or trying embarrass her in front of him. Girls need to stick together where boys are concerned. Spending your time showing him how amazing you are instead will be much more productive.

Just good friends

This can be a difficult one to judge. They talk all the time and tell each other everything, but are they more than just good friends? Well it's hard to say but your best bet is to look at her behaviour when she's with him. Does she act girlie or is she just one of the lads? If she farts/burps/makes rude jokes then she's probably the latter and he probably just sees her as another mate. If so you don't have anything to worry about and making friends with her might give you a great source of info about him.

Three's a crowd

So what about the girls in your life? Friends are pretty important and sometimes they can cause a few problems of their own when it comes to boys, like what happens when you and your best friend both fancy the same guy! Disaster, now you'll be forced to choose between the guy of your dreams and a friend of a lifetime. Which do you pick?

First you need to know whether you actually have to pick because while she might have a bit of a thing for him she might be more than happy to let you have him especially if you saw him first. But be careful that she isn't just saying that she doesn't mind when really it's going to start causing big problems between you two. If you think she's jealous then have a talk with her and encourage her to tell you how she really feels.

If she does tell you that she's upset about it or asks you to leave him alone then you need to think carefully about where your priorities lie. Generally boys come and go but friends will be there for a lot longer. How much fun would it be going out with a guy if you didn't have a friend to laugh about all the goofy things he did? It might be best to decide that both of you will keep to drooling from afar to prevent any arguments.

But that will only work if both of you keep to the bargain. If she decides to go behind your back to flirt with him then you have every right to confront her about it. If she says that she is only friends with him but you know for a fact they hadn't spoken a word to each other until you had told her you liked him then you might as well forget about him. And forget about her while you're at it!

Phew, after all the things can go wrong it wouldn't be surprising if you didn't have any boys left on your list. If that's the case then don't be afraid to start all over again at stage one, you obviously just haven't found the right one yet. If you do happen to be lucky and have someone special in mind than it's time to crank things up a little!

Turning on the flirt

By now you should be quite comfortable with being around him. Don't worry if it's still a bit awkward, he is a hottie after all so it's to be expected. But boys lose interest quickly if they think they don't have a chance so you need to start making your feelings clear and then you can find out whether he's interested in you in the same way. This is when you need to do a bit of flirting. If just the sight of that word makes you shudder, don't worry, you're not alone in not actually knowing how to "flirt". That's where this little "how to" might come in handy.

The Amateurs guide to flirting

We've all seen the cartoons where the girl bats her eyelids and suddenly she's got a flock of boys with flowers but in reality it's not that easy unfortunately. Mainly because if you've ever tried to bat your eyelids most boys will probably think you've got something caught in your eye. Flirting is really a way of behaving towards someone and you'll probably find that when you're talking to someone you fancy you do it naturally. But if you're finding it a bit difficult to get the message across here's a couple of tips to get you started before you make up some moves of your own.

Tip one: Eye contact, it's the easiest thing to do and yet extremely effective at getting your crushes attention as long as your careful it doesn't come out as more of a death stare. All you need to do is keep glancing over at him and when you finally catch his eye hold his gaze for a few seconds more than usual then look away. A minute or so later look back and do the same thing but before you look away smile at him.

Tip two: Stand a little closer to him than you would normally. Now you can give him a few subtle hints that you like him by gently touching him on the arm while you're talking.

Tip three: But if you really want him to get the idea you'll have to be confident, which boys always find sexy, because to be honest they just don't get subtle. If your feeling daring put your hand on his knee for a few seconds, perhaps while your laughing at one of his "oh so funny" jokes.

Tip four: It might seem silly but copying his actions will sub-consciously tell him you're interested. For example watch to see how he's sitting or standing and do the same. Be careful with your body language around him, crossing your arms and legs sends "keep away" however open arms, standing straight and facing towards him all give the impressions of confidence.

Tip five: Although actions do speak louder than words, what you say to him is still pretty important. It is a well known fact that guys love too think that they are funny so one of the best ways to flirt is to ALWAYS laugh at his jokes. Yes, even the lame knock knock ones that you just know he got from a prehistoric joke book. Perhaps, don't turn into hysterical laughter at every one because it could give the game away or he'll think you're being sarcastic. A little forced giggle now and then will suffice.

Tip six: Nothing says I like you like "I like your shirt". Compliment him on his clothes, after-shave, hairstyle or even his grandma and he'll be putty in your hands.

WHAT NOT TO DO WHILST FLIRTING!

A light brush with his arm is good; full on inappropriate groping is not! This includes smacking his bum, however tempting and funny it seems to be at the time.

Try not to snort while you laugh, it's just not very lady like.

Swearing can be intimidating and makes you look trashy rather than classy.

Be careful about bitching about someone to him, it makes you sound mean and it could turn out to be one of his best friends!

Use ANY of the following chat up lines …they are just too cheesy

- *Get your coat you've pulled*
- *I've lost my mobile number, can I have yours*
- *If sexy was a crime you'd be going straight to jail*
- *Aren't you tired, because you've been running through my mind all day*

Well you certainly like him and by now he should have a pretty good idea how you feel as well. Only question to ask now is...

Does he like you?

Brace yourself because this is the ultimate decider. You've let him know you're interested but now you need to know whether he feels the same way, which is tricky as when you're smitten you often mistake friendly gestures for signs of true love. Try some of these simple tests to see where his heart truly lies.

Test 1
You're sitting with him and some friends. You get up to go get some drinks for everyone and casually ask if someone could give you a hand (making sure he hears you).
He...
A jumps at the chance to help you.
B avoids looking at you and pretends not to hear whilst being "deep in conversation" with someone else.

Test 2
Mention you've been dying to see a new band but can't find anyone to go with you.
He...
A offers to go with you even though you know he's not really into that type of music.
B mutters something along the lines of "what a shame" before quickly changing the subject to last nights football score.

Test 3
Pretend to have a bit of an argument with one of your friends in front of him. Get her to storm off while you go to sit beside him and sigh.
He...
A asks you if you're ok and acts concerned but doesn't force you to tell him what the fight was about.
B doesn't even notice your little display but carries on laughing at his mate trying to burp the alphabet.

Test 4
He has a bag of sweets. Wait till there's one left then ask him for it.
He...
A after some mild protesting and perhaps flirty teasing gives it to you.
B licks it in front of your face before offering it to you with a smug grin.

Test 5
Sit by yourself where he can see you, don't text or read just look slightly bored.
He...
A leaves his friends to come talk to you and makes a bet that he can make you laugh in less than five minutes.
B ignores you completely.

Straight **A**'s?
You've certainly caught yourself a boy. Strap your high heels on and strut your smug self onto the next section.

3 or fewer **A**'s?

Ok so he's allowed to fail a few but you might want to reconsider whether he really is the right one for you. It could be that he's just shy or hasn't really had much experience about how to act in front of girls. Only you can answer whether you're doing all the running after and whether it's worth it.

B class?
 Uh oh things aren't looking to good. You could persevere but remember there are plenty more boys who might pay a lot more attention to you than this guy does and it's a lot more fun when you get to be the one who plays hard to get!

He likes you and you like him but what happens now to stop you falling into that horrible gap between strangers and couples commonly called the dreaded "just friends"? The cure, a date of course! For those of you whose heart rate is raising to alarming levels at just the thought of spending a few hours...alone...with a guy, calm down. As the well-known phrase goes on Blue Peter: here's one we did earlier!

Make it a date

He like's you and you like him but what happens now to stop you falling into that horrible gap between strangers and couples commonly called the dreaded "just friends"? The cure, a date of course! For those of you who's heart rate is raising to alarming levels at the thought of spending a few hours...alone...with a guy, calm down. As the well-known phrase goes on Blue Peter: here's one we did earlier!

Meet Gabby (er that's kind of me again). She's your average girl. Average height, an average best friend called Emily, average house with average parents and average ... (well you get the picture by now). She fancies Joe, your average hottie. While under normal circumstances it would be kept under strict lock and key, for the purposes of very important research, take a sneak peak into my diary when I ventured on my not so average first date!

Tuesday 4th
Joe was looking so particularly fab at school today, with his hair doing that floating halo thingy again, that I just couldn't bear to sit around waiting for him to be scooped up by some other girl. After deliberating it in

the toilets with Emily for the majority of lunch I finally took the plunge, strode out and just asked him if he wanted to go out with me on Saturday. Of course after preparing for this moment for the good part of an hour you'd think I might have noticed the toilet paper stuck to my shoe. But despite my red face and delightful trail of bog roll he said yes! Boy I must be good! (And modest too!)

Friday 7th
It's the night before the big day and I'm seriously panicking so I've grabbed Emily over and we've made a list of things to do in preparation:

Things to do before a date, according to Gabby and Emily

The night before:

- *Shave legs and pluck unruly eyebrows to avoid hairy-Mary traumas*

- *Ring date to find out date activities and confirm times*

- *Pick outfit. Must be comfortable and suitable for date activities.*

- *Warn friends of emergency sleepover should things go wrong!*

- *Pack equipment into handbag i.e.: make-up for touch-ups (not forgetting flavoured lip-gloss), mints, mobile, mini perfume (optional), money (not optional)*

- *Scream into pillow in excitement/fear/panic*

- *Go to bed early to compensate for pre-date insomnia*

The morning of the date:

- *Scream into pillow (again) in excitement/fear/panic*

- *Have shower using scented shampoo*

- *Get dressed*

- *Put hair into easy to manage style*

- *Apply make-up (a quick warning to all those out there who thinks this means 3 inches of foundation and half a pencil of eye liner, lots of make-up only makes boys worry about what's under it. Keep make-up fresh and light so he can see the naturally beautiful you)*

- *Ring best friend for quick pep talk*

- *Arm self with jacket, handbag and shoes*

- *Wait for doorbell!*

Saturday 8th
There I was sitting in front of the one and only Joe, with his halo-ey hair almost lifting off his perfectly formed face, my hands shaking and my heart beating so loud I

honestly thought he would hear it. It was kind of awkward at first, I couldn't seem to stop staring at him and my mind went completely blank for things to say so I grabbed the menu to at least look like I was doing something. But what to choose! I was seriously hungry and desperate for a hamburger and chips but I didn't want his first impression of me to be a greedy fat pig. So when the waiter eventually came over after what seemed like a century of sitting in silence I tried to order the salad but before I could finish Joe butted in saying, " You don't need to worry about what you eat in front of me you know. Are you sure you want that ". I couldn't believe it! Thank goodness I didn't have to spend the night munching on soggy lettuce! Afterwards he told me how he stopped going to restaurants with his last girlfriend because she made him feel so uncomfortable by ordering the smallest thing on the menu and never having dessert. I must say hearing about his ex so soon was a bit weird but whoever thought boys are actually pleased when a girl orders a bigger meal than they do!

The conversation went great for a while until I ran out of stuff to say about seedless grapes (what!). A couple minutes passed and it seemed we were heading for that dreaded silence again, the kind when a giant ball of tumbleweed comes rolling across the table. Then for some reason I decided to mutter something about how awkward it was. Fortunately he found it hilarious, for reasons unknown, and we started chatting again. Before I knew it we were all finished and it was time to pay the bill. He took out a giant wad of cash, ready to pay for the both of us. Of course I was flattered but I knew it would be totally unfair for me to make him pay it all so I offered half. He looked really grateful!

Eventually, we were back at my house. He walked me right to my door and even held my bag open for me while I tried to find my keys! But when I said that I had a great time he just stood there silent and didn't reply. I could feel the tears already. I had thought things had gone so well, how had I managed to mess it up! "Oh well his loss" I thought so I turned round to ask if he wanted me to call him or not and he planted a giant smacker right on my lips! Boy I must be really, really good!

Now that's how it's done! Dates don't have to be difficult in fact if you can overcome your nerves they can be great! The key is not to worry and to just be yourself because after all he's probably feeling just as (if not more) scared than you! If you're still worried, lets see what points we can take from this experience to make sure your date runs just as smoothly (if not better)!

Ask 2 to 3 days in advance of the day you want to go out on a date. Weekends are a good time to pick but don't feel offended if says he is busy. He might *actually* have to go and see his great grandma in Barbados.

Always check feet prior to leaving toilets for stray bog roll!

Follow the excellent to do list to be well prepared and add on anything else that you might forget to do.

Always be on time! Being late for a date sets a bad mood for the rest of the night. If you can't possibly make it on time try to phone or text him to make sure he doesn't think you've stood him up.

Order whatever you want to order! As Joe so kindly pointed out, boys like it when a girl orders a decent meal!

Avoid bringing up the subject of your exes. There's not really an explanation why, it's just one of those "unwritten rules"

If the conversation dries up try making a joke out of the awkwardness. Apparently some people find it hilarious!

Always offer to pay for your share. It's just not fair otherwise.

If the date goes badly don't worry. Put it down as practice and forget about it. It was probably his fault anyway!

However, if the date does go well, you could be faced with a drastic case of:

"To kiss or not to kiss"...

Ah to kiss or not kiss, that is the question. Whether 'tis nobler to kiss or be kissed"? Well on a first date it's probably unlikely that you and your date will be ready to kiss for the first time. Remember it is quite a big step to take and you shouldn't do it unless your 100 % certain. If a guy puts pressure on you to do anything you don't want to do, never, ever, ever give in. He's obviously a scumbag not worth your precious dating time that could be spent finding someone who will respect you.

Saying all that, it is possible that the circumstance may arise in which your date would like to kiss you and you would like to kiss him. Well you've probably been wanting to give him a big smoocher since you first laid eyes on him so here's the low down on all that kissing malarkey.

He's most likely to try to kiss you when you are alone together and probably when you are saying goodbye to one another. Therefore, when it's reaching the end of the date try giving the back of your hand a sly lick and then smelling it to check your breath. If it's a bit iffy have a couple of mints. Plus now would be a good time to put on some flavoured lip gloss as long as you can restrain yourself from licking it off beforehand!

You can probably tell that he's going to kiss you if he stops talking, gets fidgety with his hands and does quite a few nervous coughs. Should you see any of these tell tale signs, let the conversation come to a natural halt (emphasis on the natural, stopping mid sentence could cause a few concerns), turn so your facing him and look into his eyes. Hopefully he should get the hint and start leaning forwards towards you. Wait till he gets quite close and then start leaning in as well tipping your head to the side slightly so you don't bump noses! When his lips reach yours, shut your eyes, press your lips onto his a little and gently pull away and open your eyes. Small blunders could be knocking noses or teeth but if this happens just laugh it off and carry on. Afterwards give him a nice smile to show that you liked it or else he'll probably go home worrying that he did it wrong.

Of course there's no rule saying you have to kiss on the first date so if he doesn't try to kiss you it certainly doesn't mean that he doesn't like you. Probably he was just too nervous, didn't think it was the right time or didn't feel that he knew you enough. Don't take it as an insult and enjoy the date for the fun you had.

But hang on just before you head off for your own hot date, now might be a good time to think about what to wear.

Work it baby

We've all done the short skirts, skimpy tops and enough fake tan to make us glow in the dark thing and should have all learnt by now that if you're trying to wow him then keep things classy. If you're wanting to show off a bit of skin then go for either a low neckline or a skirt to show off your legs, *not both!* And if we really must fake tan then keep it to a subtle glow.

This is perfect for a first date...

A vest top with skinny jeans. Peep-toe high heels. A few gold bangles on the wrist.

Coloured tank top, simple but sexy. As a rough guide brunettes should go for deep reds, blonde goes great with emerald greens and red heads suit something in caramel or beige.

Boot cut or skinny jeans work best here and dark blue will make your legs look thinner!

Some peep-toe high heels will add that touch of glamour.

Add some statement jewellery of yours to give the outfit your own personal touch.)

Tip: swap high heels for flat pumps if you know you'll be doing a lot of walking on your date.

Quick recap

You're all ready to go but just before you head out the door here are some final pointers:

If you find yourself getting a few pre-date jitters then keep repeating to yourself "I'm hot and ready to trot", it's cheesy but it'll get you feeling more confident in no time.

On your date just try to relax and enjoy yourself, laugh at his jokes and be yourself!

If things go well, wait until the next day and give him a quick text asking if he enjoyed himself.

If he says yes then wave goodbye to stage 2 and hello onto the final part of your mission for a boyfriend!

GABBY

"NOW FOR STAGE 3"

Stage three

Title: Sealing the deal

Difficulty level: Potentially the most nerve wracking thing you've ever done but if you consider the reward it's well worth it!

Description: You know he likes you and you like him but who's going to make that oh so important first move to being more than friends

Contents:

The big question!	64
The lazy way	65
Dealing with rejection	66

For some strange reason it's seen as "traditional" for the boy to ask the girl out. Why? Who knows? Probably because people assume boys have more confidence in this department or it's seen as a bit pushy for a girl to make the first move. Which of course is completely untrue as most, if not all, guys would love for a girl to take the pressure off and pop the question first for once in a while. After all, they are just as scared of rejection and looking stupid as you are. If stars like Pink can take the plunge to ask their man out so can you.

THE BIG QUESTION!

No, we are not talking marriage but rather asking him to be your boyfriend. The moment you've been waiting for (or dreading) and now you're not sure whether you can go through with it because you're worried you'll get rejected. Be confident and cut out all those nagging doubts telling you that he couldn't possibly fancy you. Don't give up all hope before you've even asked because equally he could say yes!

Of course before any of that you actually have to get round to asking him. Unfortunately gone are the days when it was acceptable to get your friend to ask his friend to ask him if he wants to go out with you. You're going to have to be brave and do it yourself. I hear you gasp but it's really not all that bad. Just follow these instructions:

Tell him you want to talk or wait until you're alone with him. Look him in the eyes and smile, it'll give you a closer connection and if he smiles back it'll help calm your nerves.

There's not much point in trying to work "do you want to go out" into the conversation because you'll probably end up not doing it. Think about how disappointed you'll be with yourself if you don't ask him now and then just go for it. Say something along the lines of "I really like you and I was wondering if you wanted to go out with me". It helps to plan what you're going to say beforehand otherwise you could end up blabbing on, keep it quick and to the point and whatever you do try not to use any clichés or he might think you're making a joke.

There you have it, it literally is as easy as ABC and once you've done it you'll probably end up laughing at how silly you were for being so nervous. I even if he says no then at least you've had some practice for when you ask someone who will say yes.

THE LAZY WAY

Maybe you shouldn't know about this but there is another way. If, at last resort, you couldn't possibly imagine being able to ask him or you've tried and just can't get the words out then you could take the lazier approach. This means waiting for him to ask you but be warned, this really isn't the best option because you could be left waiting for a long time. He may never ask you out and you won't be able to move onto liking some one else because you'll always be wondering whether it'll ruin your chances with him. This method really only works if you have a very good idea that he's going to ask you anyway, for example if his friend has let it slip.

If you're still determined to get him to ask you then you need him thinking about you so talk to him as much as possible. If you know some of his friends, get them to mention that you quite fancy him, without making it too obvious you told them to, and to drop subtle hints that he should ask you out so he knows that if he did he wouldn't get rejected. Also, you need to make it as easy as possible for him by giving him loads of opportunities to ask you. Spend time with him alone, away from your friends and get talking about who's going out with who. Then casually ask him if he's got his eye on anyone. Just be sure to practice your shocked face when he says it is you!

If after all that you've finally bagged yourself a hottie then you can skip straight onto stage 4, although you might want to read a bit further on in case your new found skills are attracting some unwanted attention.

If he turned you down then hold your head up high and keep on reading.

Dealing with rejection

So what if he doesn't want to ride off into the sunset together? All is not lost, I repeat, all is not lost!

It may seem like a re-enactment of your worst nightmares but whatever you do don't try to persuade him to change his mind or anything else that might sound like begging. It may be tempting to start laughing and pretend it was a joke but more than likely you'll make yourself look insane. Keep your pride intact by coolly replying "Oh well, I tried", smile and try desperately to hold back the tears until you're out of sight.

It's tough but don't take it too personally, you're just not his type. That DOESN'T mean you're not an astoundingly beautiful, charismatic and all round fabulous girl. It just means he hasn't realised it yet. You will find someone you like even better and though it may not seem like it now in a year's time you'll probably struggle to even remember his name.

If you're really feeling down in the dumps, fill in the following list of all the things you didn't like about him and be brutally honest. Read it over and once you've finished you'll be wondering why you ever liked him to start with.

Get your friends to help you with this one to make it extra long!

Name of culprit: (bonus points for silly nicknames):
His worst feature:
He was annoying when:
The most embarrassing thing he did was:
He wasn't right for me because:
Robert Pattinson is so much more my type because:
My next crush is going to be:
He is better because:
The best thing about me is:

When you've completed that you'll probably realise that you're quite glad he didn't say yes anyway. But don't despair; someone else might have their eyes on you as we find out in the next section.

Who...me?

If the guy of your dreams comes over and asks you if you wouldn't mind being his girlfriend then you don't really need much instruction, say yes and keep your mouth shut tight before you start drooling over his hotness and he changes his mind. However, it could be that you being wonderful and all has attracted someone you might not have expected and you might not really want. Still, just as you would expect a guy to treat you with enough decency to turn you down in a nice way you have to do the same.

If a guy you're not really keen on comes over and asks you out do not do the following:

* *laugh in his face*
* *proclaim loudly that you'd rather run in a nettle bush naked than be seen with him*
* *make sick noises*
* *start to cry*
* *make a face of pure disgust*
* *scream and go and hide in the toilets hoping he'll just disappear*

Instead, you should listen to his very long speech about how fantastic you are, (great for a quick ego boost in the future) then try to look thoughtful and sad. Say that you are extremely flattered by his offer and you think he's a great guy but you just don't feel "that way" about him. Although you have to be careful not to hurt his feelings it's best if you make it clear to him that you don't fancy him, so you don't give him any false hope. If he won't take no for an answer tell him firmly. Whatever you do, don't fall into the trap of telling him you'll think about it in the hope that you can put off giving him an answer long enough for him to forget about it.

If you're really struggling then I suppose I could provide some help for a change. Hmm, making such gorgeous girlies ugly is tough. But I'm not afraid of a challenge. Here's some common dressing mistakes, ordinarily avoid these at all costs, but when faced with clingy boys make sure you attempt them all (and all at once for maximum impact!)

A hairy polo neck jumper with unicorn on the front. Baggy trousers that are too short at the bottom. Holey white socks pulled up over ankle.

No shoes. Crazy hair.

Dig out that "lovely" jumper your aunty sent you last Christmas.

Didn't you hear hairy polo-necks with a unicorn on the front were all the rage at the moment?

Rescue those trousers from that charity shop bag! So what if they are too short, team with white pull up socks and you're onto a winner.

No kitten heels here. Time for a flowery wellie revival I think.

Tip: just make sure you avoid any potential boyfriends, you don't want to be scaring them off as well.

Hopefully you'll now be a loved up lady and ready to embark on your most exciting stage yet, a relationship! But unfortunately these things take a bit of practice and if by now you're still a boy-free zone then don't worry, you just haven't found anyone good enough for you yet. Flick back to the start and hopefully we'll see you back here real soon!

That's stage 3 over. *Phew.*

Stage four

Title: Couple stuff

Difficulty level: All the hard work is over; this stuff is easy as pie

Description: finally, all your dreams have come true. He's yours and now you can spend all your days gazing into each other's eyes, watching the sunset together......

This chapter is just some handy hints for smoothing out those little glitches. After all boys are always going to be boys, they are always going to lie, mess up and say the wrong thing because that's what they do. but you'll grow to love them for it.

Contents:

The rules of a relationship	*71*
Date ideas	*72*
Txt messages:	*74*
Buying presents	*76*
Keeping the balance	*79*
Meeting the parents	*80*
Bring out the pearls	*83*
Boy training camp	*87*

The rules of a relationship

In case you didn't know already there are certain changes that apply when you go from "flirty friends" to "full - on couple"

-Thou shalt not blatantly stare at hot guys when with him or flirt with another guy. The days when it was a good idea to make him jealous are long gone.

-Thou shalt not cheat on him with another boy. If you're unsure whether your behavior would count as cheating ask yourself whether you would like you boyfriend to be acting the same way with another girl.

-Thou shalt accept his small faults and learn to like him just as he is. If he hasn't changed that annoying habit now then chances are he never will and he won't appreciate you trying to change him into someone he's not.

-Thou shalt understand he has other things that he needs to do in his life and allow him some time on his own without getting paranoid and checking up on what he is doing.

-Thou shalt make an effort to make things work. Relationship means a two-way partnership so don't take for granted that he'll call you every night. Call him instead.

-Thou shalt not get pressured into doing anything you don't want to do. Boys have a reputation for moving faster than girls want them to so don't be afraid to tell him to back off. If he has any respect for you he won't mind waiting till you're ready. Don't listen to any of his lies about "If you love me you would "or "all my other friends have done it with their girlfriends". Just because you are going out doesn't mean you have to do what he wants to keep him happy. If he threatens to dump you he's definitely not worth the bother so dump him first!

And for the preservation of your well being and the all round goodness of man kind:

-Thou shalt resist the temptation to buy matching his and hers T-shirts and becoming the twin (albeit with longer hair) your boyfriend never had.

Date ideas

If you thought your first date was fun wait till you try dating your boyfriend! It's all the fun of going to a fancy restaurant and being fussed over without the pressure of worrying about what to say and whether or not you have anything in your teeth. But it's only fair if you let him pick what to do once in a while. Plus it will stop him moaning as much the next time you drag him out to go dress shopping with you.

For him

Dates he would love you to suggest

Go-karting, it's fast, slightly dangerous and lets him show off his skilful (ahem) driving!

The cinema...but you pay. Although guys want you to think they are made of money it's most likely they are not. Secretly he would love you to pay so he can go spend his cash on the latest racing video game.

A football match. Girlfriend + sports = boy heaven

Round his house for a play station marathon followed by watching all Die-hard films back to back.

Swimming. He wants to show off his diving moves and you get to watch him wander round in swimming trunks. What's not to love!

Rock climbing. Grab your wellies and hike up a mountain. He'll feel like a real manly man directing you through the fog...even though you're actually lost.

For her

Dates you will love

For something a little more romantic, go for a walk in the countryside. It's simple but surprisingly fun and with the added bonus of being free!

Good old cinema, it's a classic that never gets old, especially if you can bag the back seats

If it's hot, spend the day at the beach. Cue flirty splashing in the sea and sharing chips on the pier.

If you prefer group dates, invite some other couples you're friends with and go bowling. Perfect if you haven't introduced your friends to his yet.

Have a cozy night round your house but beware of spying parents who'll find any excuse to keep a check on you

A fairground makes for a great date but unfortunately they tend to only come round once a year, so mark it on your calendar!

Shopping. It maybe one of your favorite past times but it's probably not his. Let him visit some of his shops and he'll soon come round to the idea.

Txt msgs...what they really mean

Boyfriends are confusing at the best of times, but put a mobile in their hand and they become tougher than a Rubik's Cube! Luckily you're looking at your own personal boy code decipher.

"Hi cnt w8 2 c u, wat time d u want 2 meet?"

If he uses shortened slang, it's not because he can't really be bothered to text; he probably just thinks it makes him look cooler.

"Ok, i'll text u soon babe"

Using a pet name shows he wants to get closer to you and although it may seem a bit cheesy it's his way of showing affection.

"Just thought I would say good night"

Sending a sweet, random text means he must besotted with you because you're always on his mind.

"Where r u I tried ringing 3 times and you didn't answer, make sure you text back this time"

However, if he always wants to know what you're doing or who you're with it's a sign he doesn't trust you. Being concerned is ok, being possessive isn't and it's a sign the relationship isn't working

"Wud it b ok if I kissed u?"

At first your probably thinking this is extremely naff, but boys aren't really the self-assured, smooth talkers they are made out to be in the films. Making the first move is hard so give him some reassurance he's not going to be rejected.

"I'll c u 2morrow then xxxx"

Putting kisses on the end of his messages is trying to show that he really cares about you so send him some back.

"Well, I think you are very beautiful"

Writing out texts in full means that he is trying to be romantic and doesn't want his message to be taken the wrong way.

"I love you"

When boys say these three words you know he means business. Don't panic if it takes him awhile to say it. When he eventually does he'll really mean it.

Buying presents

Think your dad is hard to buy for? Well it's nothing compared to trying to find that perfect present for your boyfriend. How much do you spend? What sort of card do you send? What do you buy him!

Decide with your boyfriend a limit to spend on each other so you don't have the horror of getting a diamond necklace when all you sent him was a T-shirt you picked up from a car boot sale!

Now comes the problem of exactly what to buy. Buying a joke present could be a good idea but it all depends on your guy and what sort of occasion it is. Generally it's best to stick to the usual stuff because whilst he might expect a fart cushion from his mate, it's probably not the sort of thing he wants from his girlfriend. But not all boys are the same so if you really want to put some thought into it then take the following test to find out what kind of guy he is and get a present that he'll love.

You're out shopping and while you're eyeing up the dresses you've noticed that he's done a disappearing act into the shop next door. Which shop do you find him in?

A Gap for men
B Sports world
C HMV
D Oxfam

On a Saturday you're most likely to find him:

A down the gym
B playing football with his mates
C practicing his guitar
D helping his mum with the shopping

You're planning a cozy night in front of the television and since he's paying you decide you'll let him pick the film. What film does he pick?

A Die Hard
B Rocky Balboa
C School of Rock
D The Matrix

He's taking you to a fancy restaurant. You go to meet him but he's not ready yet! What does he get caught up doing?

A gelling his hair to perfection
B watching the last five minutes of the match
C loading songs onto his i- pod
D giving advice to his friend who's having "girl troubles"

If you picked mostly:

A
Sometimes you wonder if he spends more time worrying about the way he looks then you do. He takes a lot of pride in his appearance so a present is going to make him look good is a must.

Big spender- a designer shirt. If you're not sure which colour he'll like go for white because it goes with anything.

It's the thought that counts- Cufflinks

B
This guy loves all things active and doesn't like to stay in one place all the time, so get him something that will keep up with his hectic lifestyle!

Big spender- tickets to a sports event. Preferably a game involving his favorite team. If you don't like sports yourself then if they aren't too expensive get two tickets and let him take a friend.

It's the thought that counts- sports bag

C
Your guy really loves his music and it's rare to see him without his earphones in so head down to the music shop for his perfect present.

Big spender-tickets to see his favorite band. If they aren't playing in your area any time soon have a look on e-bay for any memorabilia you can get your hands on such as signed photos of the band etc.

It's the thought that counts- mixed tape of all the songs you know he likes.

D
He's thoughtful and sensitive so make sure your present to him really means something and he'll be sure to cherish it.

Big spender- a watch with a special message (like the date of when you started going out) engraved on the inside.

It's the thought that counts- a cool keyring with a picture of you two together in it.

Receiving a bad present... and making it look good

Uh oh, perhaps he doesn't know you as well as you think he does when you realize he's gotten you a frilly pair of gloves that you could probably take onto the antiques road show instead of the CD you'd been shamelessly hinting for. First things first, however hideous the present may be it's still a present so you're going to have to give your best shot at making it look like you're grateful. Give him a hug so you can let out those few tears of disappointment behind his back. Try to look a little enthusiastic about it but don't overdo it or he'll guess and he'll probably be really hurt because he spent ages trying to get the perfect present.

Obviously he wasn't listening to the subliminal messages you were sending in the shop so next time a special occasion comes up tell him what you would really like. That way you take the pressure off him to try and choose something and there won't be any nasty surprises on the big day!

Friends

Keeping the balance

A new relationship is always exciting but being so besotted with a boy can make you forget about still making an effort with your friends. For those friends who don't have a boyfriend of their own it can be difficult for them to understand that you have someone else you need to spend time with and they can feel pushed aside. Do the following to keep the balance:

When you talk to her try to discuss other things other than what sweet thing your boyfriend just bought you etc. Talk about things you're both interested in so she feels included in the conversation.

If they don't know each other, introduce you boyfriend and your best friend to each other properly. If they are friends you can go out places with both of them so you don't need to split your time as much.

However don't be tempted to take him every time your friends ask you to go somewhere. Shoe shopping should be girls only!

If your friend has a boyfriend of her own then try double dating. If not ask your boyfriend if he has a single friend he can bring with him.

If time is short give your friends a call or quick text instead, just to show you still care.

If you're having a big night out with your boyfriend which your friends aren't going to then invite them for a trip to the salon the day before to help with the beauty preparations and catch up on the gossip.

Meeting the Parents

It's bound to happen sometime, whether it is a quick hello or a long formal meal if things are getting really serious. Whichever, meeting the parents is always a big deal. You get to see what your boyfriend might look like in 20 years or so and they get to grill you about...well pretty much everything. It's scary and it's awkward but once the initial meeting is over you'll probably find it's not that bad. So next time you're invited for a meal with the parents make sure you brush up on the following guide for a winning first impression:

Parent proof guide to etiquette

Saying hello: Make sure you say hello with one of those giant, fake cheesy grins and be looking to see if they want to shake hands because some parents weirdly think that's a good thing to do. If you're having a meal with them then for extra credit bring them a nice bottle of wine.

Small talk: Before they get into the deep stuff they'll probably ask you some random questions about the weather and things like that just to break the ice. Try to sound polite and where possible answer with a bit more than "yes" and "no" so they know you're listening.

The serious stuff: It's only a matter of time before they get down to asking you some personal questions. It's not a good idea to make up massive lies like about how you love classical music so much you spent you entire Christmas money on a Mozart collection just to get them to like you. But no one said you couldn't elaborate on the truth and perhaps forgetting to mention getting detention for making out in the school corridor wouldn't be the worst thing. As long as it sounds like a likely story and there's no chance you could get found out, what's the harm?

A lasting impression: As we all know, flattery really does get you everywhere. Compliment them on the food, their carpet and even the hideous green decorations that look like leftovers from Halloween. Sound genuine and they will love you for it.

Saying goodbye: Thank them for a lovely time/food that makes you appreciate McDonalds/helping you to overcome insomnia with their lecture on modern art and flash them a smile. Afterwards DO NOT start complaining to your boyfriend how boring / weird / insane his parents are. He may laugh along at the time but deep down he'll be hurt and he could go back and tell his parents what you said which wouldn't go down well. Instead comment on how nice they were, especially his mum (since all boys are mummy's boys deep down) and he'll be chuffed.

Good dinner topics

* *Your family (leave out the mad ones though).*
* *Your plans for future holidays.*
* *Your grandma's favorite recipes.*
* *The last book you read.*
* *The time you spent helping an old lady across the road(or what ever else charity-like thing you did).*
* *Most importantly...How wonderful their son is!*

Bad dinner topics

* *When you skived off school because you forgot to do your homework.*
* *All the reasons why you think television is better than reading books.*

* *Any potentially embarrassing stories that might reveal their "angel of a son to be not so angelic after all.*
* *All rude or disgusting jokes that involve things like excrement or bodily functions etc.*

So you know what to say and you know what not to do but what do you wear?

BRING OUT THE PEARLS

I'm all for originality but when it comes to meeting the parents you need to tone it down a little. All t-shirt slogans (like "I'm with stupid"), facial piercings and skyscraper heels are banned.

So buttoned up cardigan with shirt collar poking out at neckline, pencil skirt that falls below the knee. Flat round toed shoes. Bun in hair.

Nice, conservative cardigan should do. In some sort of pastel colour and yes, you do have to do up the top button.

Remember the reaction your own parents had when you started putting your hair into a Mohican?

Chances are his parents won't take too fondly to it either. Whatever happened to the good old plait anyway?

The general rule of thumb with shoes here is that if your grandma owns a pair then wear them. In fact why not just borrow a pair of hers!

If he's meeting your parents

Parents can be embarrassing at the best of times but there's something about meeting a boyfriend that makes them crank up their cringe-o-meter full scale. A quick low down on what they can and can't say might be a good idea to avoid too many please-let-the-ground-open-up-and-swallow-me-whole-right-now worthy moments later on. Here are a few things you might want to suggest:

My suggestions: by your loving daughter (who never once told your boss his wig wasn't on properly when he came round for tea).

Please do not try to be funny. No knock-knock jokes, pranks or funny stories about what you did when you were young.

Refer to me at all times by my proper name, no "poochy-kins" allowed!

Whatever you do, keep all photos, videos and teddy bears well away. (For extra safety lock them in a cupboard)

Do not ask him any horrible questions like "what are your intentions with our daughter".

He won't be impressed by extensive knowledge of the Amazonian rainforest and please don't try to be clever by discussing politics.

Don't try out any of your "lingo" and trying to be "cool". Just be parents, er... normal parents.

Show your parents this list beforehand and make them sign a piece of paper saying that if they don't keep to all the rules on the page they have to give you £20. If they refuse to sign the piece of paper tell them that if they don't you won't bring any of your future boyfriends home and you don't know what kind of boy you'll go out with next. Give them a devious look and they'll be signing that paper quicker than you can say "knock-knock"

When he does arrive, help him out by introducing him properly. And try not to laugh at his goofy gelled hair and ironed tie. It'll be important to him that your parents like him so he'll be making a big effort.

If you notice he's finding it difficult to join in the conversation think of something you can all talk about and encourage him to join in by asking him a question. No doubt he'll be a bit tongue-tied so fill in any awkward silences for him to take the pressure off. If your parents should break the rules you set for them laugh it off and change the subject quickly. When his back is turned give them an evil glare and rub your fingers together like you've got money in them. They will soon remember their manners!

Lastly, don't worry if suddenly he doesn't want to come and talk to you because he is discussing football with your dad. Leave them to it, it's a male bonding thing that girls will never understand.

If things go badly

Uh oh, nothing can put a strain on a relationship like your parents not liking your boyfriend. Perhaps they think he is too old, too immature or maybe they aren't used to the fact that their once little girl is now in a relationship. Whatever it is it's important that you find out exactly why they aren't so keen on him after all. Sit down and have a chat with them, tell them of all his good points and try to put their worries at rest. Hopefully they should agree to give him another chance and try to get along with him. If so why not invite him bowling with your family or something a little less formal so everyone can feel a bit more relaxed and they can see the real him. It might just mean that they need a little more time to get used to him.

If they are still adamant that they don't want you to go out with him then maybe you should think about whether they actually have a point. Although it sometimes seems that your parents go out of their way to ruin your fun, generally they are only doing it because they care and think it's the best thing for you. After all you'll probably find that your mum has had her fair share of boyfriends in the past and can spot a rotten one a mile off.

Boy training camp

So the first few weeks of your relationship were amazing. But after a couple of month's it feels like the fireworks are fizzling out! Sound familiar? Well it doesn't mean that you made the wrong decision and you don't like him anymore, it's just you'll be getting to know the real him as he gets more comfortable with you. That means you'll see what he's like when he's not drenched in after shave and hair gel. But that's not necessarily a bad thing because you'll also be a lot closer and you can see him without having to worry for days about what you're going to wear and buying a whole new outfit. However if you do feel that the relationship isn't as good as it used to be don't be hasty and dump him. Send your boy to training camp and you'll be guaranteed to rekindle your love!

Boy goes in: Prince Charming comes out

So you want him to be more... CARING

You want him to: Turn off the footy and have a long, meaningful talk about feelings and stuff.

He: Notices that you're bored so attempts to explain the offside rule to you in the hope you'll all of a sudden become remotely more interested...which of course you don't and it in fact adds to your boredom.

How to change it... Next time he's watching the football, pull out your mobile and start texting a friend. Pretend like you're so deep in conversation that you don't hear what he's says to you and laugh a couple of times like they've said something funny. When he glances over to see what you're sending hide the phone like you don't want him to see it. He'll be so curious about it, he'll forget all about the television.

... EXCITING

You want him to: Be more inventive with dates and to treat you to somewhere special.

He: Invites you over to his house for the 5th time in a row to watch Eastenders.

How to change it: He could just have no imagination so think of where you would like him to take you and suggest it to him. If he still doesn't take the hint then every time he invites you round make up an excuse that you have to go somewhere but ask him if he wants to come. Eventually he'll get so sick of not seeing you that he'll have to come out of the house.

... THOUGHTFUL

You want him to: Be the first one to text and send you sweet messages saying how special you are to him.

He: Hardly ever texts you first and when he does it's to tell you about how he managed to set fire to his own fart.

What to do: Act aloof and get him to chase you for a change. If you're always the one to get in touch he'll think he doesn't have to make any more effort. Instead don't text him for awhile and when he finally gets in touch with you don't reply straight away. When you do send short one liners, he'll be begging for your attention in no time!

... ROMANTIC

You want him to: Whisper in your ear, hold your hand, give you a cuddle, kiss your cheek, and peck you on the lips…. Then snog

He: Goes straight in for a snog with no consideration he's just downed a curry and coke.

What to do: Try to set a more romantic mood when you're alone. (Unfortunately there's not much you can do about him when he's with his friends because he'll want to come across as "Mr Cool" so expect him to act like a total pig! It's just what guys do.) Invite him round to your house and rent a really sloppy film. Dim the lights or get a few candles to set the mood and cuddle up on the sofa. If he simply lunges for you, pull away quicker than you would normally and keep saying "aww" at the romantic bits in the film, so he gets the hint that's how he should be acting.

Congratulations, you and your newly transformed boyfriend have just graduated from boy training camp.

Recognise your achievements by making yourself a certificate and displaying it for all to see. (Well except your boyfriend because he might not be too happy about the real reason he had to watch Titanic instead of Terminator)

Stage Five

Title: When it all goes wrong

Difficulty level: That really all depends just how bad things have got.

Description: Now there comes a time in everyone's relationship when things aren't as rosy as they used to be. Sometimes it's just because you're going through a bad patch and others because you're not quite as suited as you used to be. Well it's important to know the difference to save time and tears!

Contents:

How to have an argument, and win!	90
Commonly known as sympton & cure	91
Cooking up a booting	99
Getting dumped	101
Moving on	101
New girlfriend? I've got new shoes.	105

How to argue and win! ...The old fashioned way

Everyone goes through a tough patch once in a while. It's virtually impossible for two people to spend a lot of time with each other and not fall out. A little argument doesn't mean that things are over, in fact it's good to clear up anything that's been bothering you otherwise it will continue to build up over time. If something is annoying you, tell him you want to talk to him and do this in person so there is no chance of things you say being taken the wrong way. Tell him in a calm manner what's upsetting you, why it upset you and what you want him to do to put things right. With such a kind request as that how can he complain? Well back in the day a true gentleman would apologize and promise not to do it again, not to mention by you a big present to really get back into your good books. But nowadays boys seem to have forgotten their manners and aren't so chivalrous. If your boy is behaving a little badly try the following remedies, tried and tested for generations. (Kind of)

Commonly known as Symptoms & Cure

The silent treatment: (Inability to talk) Tell him you are ready to talk things through when he is.

Huffiness: (Mumbling, permanent frown on face) Explain he is being childish and things would be a bit better if you could sort your problems out in a civilized manner.

Temper tantrum: (Shouting, scowl on face. Reacts very badly to being poked) Leave well alone until he has calmed down.

Weeper: (Crying/sobbing/wailing, hands in front of face trying to preserve masculinity) Soothe with calming words and stroking of the hand. After all you must have the poor thing distraught. When he's calmed down ask him to apologize if he hasn't already done so.

The fool: (Laughing a lot, doesn't take anything you say seriously. Rather annoying). Restate your reasons for being upset to him. If symptoms persist, walk away until he has decided to take more notice.

Waster: (Insults you, tells you of all the other girls he could get) Give him the boot *(that's dumped in modern day language)*

IF YOU WERE IN THE WRONG

Of course this is a very rare occurrence but even the best of us can get things wrong from time to time and it is important that we own up to our mistakes if we expect our boyfriends to do the same. The fact that generally we don't make mistakes and if we did it was because of something they had done to provoke us, is besides the point.

Tell him that you take full responsibility for whatever it was you did and that you are aware that it upset him. Then you need to say that you are very sorry for it and that you promise not to do it again.

If he accepts your apology then allow him one to two days to be grumpy with you. Any longer than that and he is just stringing it out to make you feel bad. Don't allow him to use it as a bargaining tool to make you do things. You've given an apology and that's all the compensation he is entitled to.

If he doesn't accept your apology then there isn't really anything more you can do. You'll just have to wait until he is ready to forgive you. In the meantime give him a little time by himself so he can think things through. Don't pester him with sorry notes and endless phone calls, you'll only make him more annoyed.

However knowing that we were in the wrong is different to allowing a boy to convince you it was your fault when you know deep down it wasn't. If you know you were right then don't back down otherwise it will cause even more problems later on.

Is he cheating?

Could the problems in your relationship be down to the involvement of someone else? Has something happened to make you suspect he could be cheating on you? Well before you start throwing round accusations you need to make sure you have your facts right otherwise you could cause some serious issues about trust which could permanently damage your relationship. You're going to need your spyglass because you'll need to go on the search for some evidence:

Calling you by someone else's name. Once is a silly mistake, twice and he's got some explaining to do, especially if it's the same name.

He stops seeing you as much because he always has plans with his "friends". Talk to his friends to see if he has actually been going out with them but be aware they could be covering for him.

He tells you he's going out shopping with his mother, but you see him waiting around outside the cinema. A quick interrogation is in order, if you think he's lying about where he is going then ask him about his plans before he goes. Make a note of what he says and then ask him the same questions when he gets back. Are the answers the same?

He smells of another girls perfume and his lips look distinctly more red than usual. Either that or he's just very in touch with his feminine side.

He never has any credit on his phone but you see him top up every week. If you can have a look through his call logs, has he been ringing a mysterious number more than once?

Once armed with all your evidence and you've made up your mind that you have something to worry about then the next thing to do is to confront him about it. Ask him to explain some of the funny things you've noticed have been happening. If you're happy he has a genuine excuse then all is good, if not tell him what you suspect he's been up to.

Careful how you say this though, tell him what you're concerned about but don't make it sound like your mind is made up about him cheating on you in case you are wrong. If he can't explain himself or he confesses all then it's time to send him packing. He'll probably beg you to forgive him and tell you that he will finish it with her, but remember if he wasn't honest first time around then you have no reason to trust anything else he says. Boys who aren't happy with just the one girl are a recipe for disaster so you should stay well away.

You think you like someone else

If you're thinking about cheating yourself then you'd better stop and take a good long look at yourself in the mirror. Do you really want to be known as a two-timing liar? No, of course you don't but that's exactly the sort of reputation you'll get if you start messing around with someone else whilst still in a relationship. It's not fair and it will only end in tears, so don't do it.

Think about whether you really like this other person or whether it's just the temptation of something you can't have. The grass always looks greener on the other side and most likely you think you like someone else because there's problems with the relationship you're in. Examine them first and try to fix them. If they can't be fixed then maybe it's time to think about ending it. But whatever you do, don't begin something with someone else until you've fully ended the relationship with the person you're with.

You just don't like him anymore

You were the perfect couple and there was a time when he could do no wrong. But now that little habit of his you used to find adorable is becoming increasingly irritating and you're beginning to forget exactly why you're going out with this guy. Perhaps it's time to think about ending it all...

But don't rush into things, if you've made the wrong decision it can be extremely hard to get them back again. Think about why you want to dump him.

If he's horrible to you, makes you feel bad about yourself, hits you, tries to pressure you into things you don't want to do, threatens you, tries to control your life (in an obsessive way) or in any way makes you upset then don't hesitate to chuck him.

Not everything is that serious. Sometimes you just don't like someone as much as you used to anymore. Maybe your interests have changed or he's just not what you expected when you first said yes. Relationships are supposed to be fun, when it's not there's not much point.

However you might think that you're not that keen but remember no one is perfect, you only think some people are because you don't know them enough to know their faults.

Don't dump him because you think he's going to dump you, you could very easily have got the wrong idea. Talk to him about it before you jump into something you'll probably regret.

Getting rid of boys

If you're sure you want to get rid of him and you've given yourself time to think it through and you still haven't changed your mind then you need to start thinking about how to end it. You could try the following:

Looking rank, wear baggy clothes, forget to put your make-up on, don't wash your hair...etc

Most guys have a fear of commitment so casually mentioning one of these should the trick:

The baby names you've thought about to call your children - mention at least seven

What color you want for your wedding dress and your designs for your dream house including a nursery

What things you want him to leave you in his will

Being extremely clingy will soon get on his nerves, and yours as well probably.

And if all else fails telling him about your arguments with the "voices in your head" will send him running for the hills.

But of course they are a little harsh and not to mention time consuming so obviously you are going to do it the proper way. After all, even though you might not fancy him any more, he still deserves some respect. (Unless you are dumping him because he has done something very bad, which in that case you are free to end it in whatever way you see fit.)

I thought now might be a good time to revisit my diary and show you what became of the Joe saga.

Thursday 22nd
There is a limit to just how much enjoyment a girl can get from looking at a boy's perfectly coiffed hair. Now that Joe has admitted to me his secret is Pantene Pro V and a weekly deep wax treatment (yes, I have seen the hair net), I'm just not sure I find it all that attractive any more. What's more I think that the fact he'll let me borrow is hair straighteners, which do a wonderful job on my fringe, is the only reason we are together any more. I used to think the little snort he did when he laughed was kind of cute but now its reached fog horn level and I swear I can hear him within a 2 mile radius. Maybe it's not that, maybe it's the fact that when we went to a party yesterday, I couldn't even dance with Emily without him clinging to my side and attempting to do the Beyonce butt wobble to try and fit in. I suppose

I should be grateful that I have a boyfriend who wants to fit in with my friends but his face was so serious and I'm a bit worried he actually thought the dance move looked good. Plus, there's just some times when you want to be with girls, just girls. Like the shopping trip for dresses we have planned for next Saturday which he has begged me to let him come to for the past week, saying "I'll sit outside the changing rooms and shout my opinion in". Sure, because that will be fun...

Maybe I'm just being picky, I'll give it another week to think about it.

Friday 3rd
The boy has got to go! I told him a joke I heard today and he laughed (aka. Snorted) in my ear so loud, it's still ringing. If I don't want to have tinnitus for the rest of my life, I'm just going to have to sacrifice the relationship.

Saturday 4th
Not the most pleasant of experiences, I'll admit, but it wasn't altogether as bad as I had thought. I couldn't think of any good reason that we should break up, apart from for the sake of my hearing, so I said that he was a great guy but I was too busy with other things in my life to have a boyfriend at the moment. I could see he was about to start with all the reasons why we could still make it work so I beckoned secretly to Emily to send out my plan B. Plan B was a random girl from my school and as she walked past I gave her a long look and raised my eyebrows in appreciation. Joe caught on. "Oh right! I never would have known you, err, swung that way. Well it's great you've found yourself" he said to which I just smiled and let him think what he liked. Ok, so I'm a coward but it ended in him giving me a hug and wishing me all the best! No harm done and

on the way home we met up with Plan B's brother. Not that I would possibly be thinking about tying myself up in another relationship but where is my red lipstick...

COOKING UP A BOOTING.

If you're sure he's as dull as an Antiques Roadshow omnibus then you better give him the heave ho.

INGREDIENTS

A heap of firmness
A squeeze of calmness
Some comforting friends
A sure mind
A pinch of alone time (face to face!)
Some tears and tissues to garnish

Whatever you do, DO NOT dump him via the following: email, text, a note shoved in his letter box, his mum, your best friend or his best friend. It may seem the easy way out but it's heartless and getting a reputation for being cruel may put off other potential boyfriends.

You're just going to have to pluck up the courage and do it face to face. Looking a little less than glamorous (i.e. minging) while you doing it may help soften the blow.

Make sure he's on his own and you're not having an argument. Doing it in the heat of a row might make him think that you don't actually mean it.

Give the old line "we need to talk" and then carry on along the lines of "things haven't been going very well lately"..."I don't think its working"..."I want to split".

Make sure you don't say, "I think we should split up" because that's giving him an option and he might try to persuade you otherwise.

If he asks for a reason it's going to take some seriously quick thinking and lying as saying "I just don't fancy you anymore" is a bit of a slap in the face. Of course you could just memorize the following:

I want different things now

I need to concentrate on schoolwork for the moment

My parents have decided not to let me have a boyfriend until I'm at least 30

I'm moving to Australia

Finish off with "I still want to be friends" and you're done. If he starts to cry/beg/attach himself to your foot gently tell him you're sorry, look really sad then run for it and avoid talking to him for the next few weeks. Don't feel you have to take him back just because he went all puppy-eyes on you.

Avoid going out with anyone else for at least the next three weeks or just don't flaunt your new boyfriend right in front of him.

Beware of any nasty rumors about you spread round by his mates/evil glares from his mum when you bump into her at the shops/seeing him with a hundred different girls in an attempt to make you see what you're missing. Whatever he tries stand your ground and he'll be over it in no time.

Getting dumped

There's always the possibility he will dump you first, however unlikely it may seem, and the truth is there's no easy way around it...it hurts. If he was genuinely nice about it then respect his decision, perhaps you just couldn't see what problems there were or it might have been other things in his life that made the relationship difficult. It doesn't mean you're no longer attractive to all boys and you're destined to be a spinster with nine cats.

However if he did it in a horrible way you officially have the right to tell everyone just how nasty he was and that he keeps a teddy rabbit locked away in his bottom drawer.

Moving on

You got dumped and everything sucks. Everyone knows the feeling and it's not very good. But you won't be upset about it forever, honest! Stick to the moving on plan and you'll be out of those fluffy pajamas in a jiffy.

Day 1-4

Assign yourself 4 days to sit at home and wallow in self-pity. Grab some chocolate, DVD's and tissues and cry...all night if you must.

Make sure you aren't tempted to ring him and say something you might regret by switching off your phone and hiding it away somewhere. Mums are especially good at this time so it might be nice to have a good heart to heart with her and tell her how you feel.

They can be surprisingly good at making you feel better and perhaps you could even persuade her to make you a "poor me" hot chocolate.

Recipe for "poor me" hot chocolate

Put three teaspoons of cocoa powder into a tall mug.

Fill the mug with hot, full-creamed milk, stirring as you pour.

Crumble in half a chocolate flake, leave a few seconds to melt then give the drink another stir.

Top with whipped cream, mini marshmallows and the remaining flake.

Take two to three times a day, with vast amounts of sweets and ice cream.

Day 5-7

Invite your friends around to comfort you and join you in your misery. Spend at least 2 hours talking about the teddy he still has in his bedroom and generally making fun of him. You'll probably find out what your friends actually thought about him and it might surprise you that most likely they didn't like him that much either.

This is also the time he is most likely to ring and ask you to forgive him because he has made a big mistake. Think about whether you actually want him back and don't feel like you have to. Maybe you have realized that things weren't as good as they seemed. However it could be that he genuinely did make a mistake and if you miss him as much as he is missing you then it's ok to take him back. He'll just have some serious groveling to do.

Day 8-10

Chuck away the tissues. A few outbursts are allowed but other than that keep crying to a minimum. Fill your time with shopping trips, pamper days and anything else that's all to do with you.

Unfortunately, this could also be the time you find out about his new girlfriend, which could knock you a little. Remind yourself of all the things he did to annoy you and all the reasons why you are glad you aren't going out with him anymore. If he or his friends ask you how you feel about it then just tell them that you're happy for them. At least then you'll look like you're not bothered. If it helps pull out all your old posters of hot celebrities and hang them all over your room to remind you that they're are plenty more fish in the sea.

Day 11-14

You're now ready to truly move on. You might want to consider getting rid of some of the things that remind you of him if you but don't be too quick to throw it all away because you might want to keep it to look back on when you're older. Plus it's always a fun party game to pull out your old love letters and read them aloud in a highly dramatic voice. Keep a few things in a box of sentimental things and chuck the rest away. If you have any of his CD's or DVD's give them to one of his friends or yours to pass on to him if you don't think you're up to talking to him yourself.

If you find yourself feeling a little down sometimes just remember that you are single now and ready to find someone even hotter/cuter/sexier than the last one.

"GIRLS RULE" SLEEPOVER

Catch up on lost time with your friends and have a sleepover to celebrate your new boy free life!

*   Decorate the room in pink, glitter and all things girly. Bring down all your fluffy pillows and teddy bears and put them amongst the sleeping bags.

*   Serve a buffet with little sandwiches and pizza slices on a silver platter. For drinks have grape juices in tall wineglasses and desert should be a big bowl of melted chocolate with marshmallows and strawberries for dipping.

*   Watch romantic films with hot guys in and discuss which actor had the best bum afterwards.

*   Party games include confessing your most embarrassing crushes, drawing cartoons of people in your school and friends must guess who they are and singing karaoke in your funniest voice.

*   Aim to stay up as late as possible discussing gossip and secrets. Those who fail to stay awake past 12 must have something drawn on their face whilst they are asleep.

*   In the morning serve guests with breakfast in bed. A big plate of toast and jam will go down a treat.

* As a reminder of your wonderful party, hand out pin badges with "Girls rule, boys drool" on them (or make up your own logo) which must be worn the following Monday to spur mid lesson laughter fits.

Ready to start the whole thing again? Relationships are great like that because once one has ended you can start up another one with someone completely new and no two are the same. So there's no reason to think whatever went wrong in your last relationship will affect your next one. Put it down as a bad experience and move on. Here's a final word on style for getting yourself looking fabulous again.

New girlfriend? I've got new shoes.

Been dumped, cheated on or just ready to show the world a whole new (single) you?

Shorts and military style jacket. High heel red shoes.

You know those short shorts he didn't like you to wear in public because he got very jealous? Pull them on and feel free to roll them up if they are just not short enough.

Military style jacket is high fashion. Show him who is boss!

Like to wear trainers? Fine. High heel kind of girl? Fine. You can wear what you want now because the only person you need to please is you!

Get your own back by upping the glamour and strutting your stuff in a tailored jacket and oversized sunnies.

Tip: Now you're looking like a diva you need to act like one too. Walk everywhere fast like you've got somewhere more important to go to and scribble little notes down on a few post it notes. He'll soon get the idea that you've got more important things going on than worrying about him.

Bye for now

And that is all there is too it. Sadly we've come to the end of the five stages and seen it all. You should be all clued about how to get your man, hold onto him and chuck him when the time is right. But it's not all about boys you know, the single life can be great fun too so enjoy it!

Take the chance to focus on some other areas in your life like hobbies, your friends or er, schoolwork. *Pfft,* as if.

When you find yourself interested in the boy world, head on back to stage one to start the fun all over again.

Who knows, maybe the next will be a keeper!

BYE

Disclaimer: I officially cannot take any responsibility for any unwanted oversized teddy bears, soppy love letters or tacky jewelry. They're inevitable side effects.

Anyone bagging a Taylor Lautner look-alike, I will take absolute blame for. *GABBY*

The End Bit

With many thanks to **Rachel Cotterill** for her technical help with the proof reading, (it was needed!) please visit her website **www.rachelcotterill.com** to see details of her own books.

Did you like all the fantastic drawings? Well they were done by the soon to be famous Manga Artist
Heby Sim.
To see more of her artwork & other books she has illustrated Visit:
www.chocolatemanga.com

A lot of girl-kind hard work has gone into creating this little book so the legal stuff is:
All rights reserved. No part of this publication may be reproduced, stored in a retrieval system, or transmitted in any form or by any means without prior permission from the publishers.

Hi I'm Heby

That's it .. Bye

Gabby

(a.k.a. **Rachel Hill** Author)

See me at: **www.gabby-guides.com**